To J.G. and the whole
Half Dome / Point Reyes group.

Thank you to Steven Haddock from MBARI
for his expertise and guidance!

Greystone Kids / Greystone Books Ltd.
greystonebooks.com

Cataloguing data available from Library and Archives Canada
ISBN  978-1-77164-888-2 (cloth)
ISBN  978-1-77164-889-9 (epub)

Editing by Kallie George
Copyediting by Dawn Loewen
Proofreading by Becky Noelle
Jacket and text design by Sara Gillingham Studio
Scientific review by Steven Haddock, PhD, Senior Scientist and Marine Biologist,
http://biolum.eemb.ucsb.edu/

Printed and bound in China on FSC® certified paper at Shenzhen Reliance Printing.
The FSC® label means that materials used for the product have been responsibly sourced.

The illustrations in this book were rendered in Adobe Photoshop.

Greystone Books thanks the Canada Council for the Arts, the British Columbia Arts Council,
the Province of British Columbia through the Book Publishing Tax Credit, and the Government of Canada
for supporting our publishing activities.

Greystone Books gratefully acknowledges the xʷməθkʷəy̓əm (Musqueam),
Sḵwx̱wú7mesh (Squamish), and səlilwətaɬ (Tsleil-Waututh) peoples on
whose land our Vancouver head office is located.

# LUMINOUS

## Living Things
## That Light Up the Night

JULIA KUO

GREYSTONE KIDS

GREYSTONE BOOKS · VANCOUVER / BERKELEY / LONDON

When it's dark out,

we need light to see.

*Light* is a kind of energy that our eyes can see.
Some light sources are natural, like the sun and fire.
Other sources of light, like light bulbs, are created by people.

But what if your body could make its own light?

When a living creature, like a firefly,
produces light, it is called *bioluminescence*.
Bioluminescent creatures make the light through
special chemical reactions inside their bodies.

You could gleam on the forest floor

Foxfire, or fairy fire, is light made by bioluminescent
fungi growing and glowing on rotting wood.

or shimmer inside a shadowy cave.

The glowworms of New Zealand and Australia
are actually young insects that will grow up and
turn into flies. They are the only bioluminescent
creatures in the world that live in caves.
These glowworms dangle sticky
glowing strands to catch insects to eat.

Just imagine . . .

# You could use your light to
# dazzle the deepest ocean depths

The deep-sea anglerfish dangles a bioluminescent ball
like a fishhook to lure smaller fish into its mouth.
These fish live deep in the ocean where no sunlight reaches.
It would be totally dark there without bioluminescence.

or to startle and distract your enemies

Vampire squid, named for their cape-like arms,
release a glowing blue cloud from their arm tips when
they're being chased. The cloud confuses their *predators*
(the creatures that are hunting the squid to eat them),
helping the squid to escape into the darkness.

Dragonfish shine a red light that only they can see to find *prey*
(the smaller fish that they hunt and eat) in the dark ocean.

or even to find a snack!

You could shine your light to call for help

The crown jellyfish uses light like a burglar alarm by
creating many bright blue flashes when it is attacked.
These flashes attract bigger fish and give the
jellyfish a chance to escape. More than half of all jellyfish
protect themselves by producing light.

or to hide in plain sight.

The jeweled squid gradually changes its brightness depending on the time of day. Matching the sunlight or moonlight coming from the surface above makes it hard for predators looking up from below to see the squid. When animals blend into their surroundings to avoid being seen, it is called *camouflage*.

And you'd be just one of *trillions* of living things that can make their own light.

Scientists think that there may be more bristlemouth lightfish, a tiny deep-sea fish, in the world than any other animal with a backbone! They use bioluminescent light for camouflage and to coordinate swimming together in a school.

Can you imagine?

Such creatures are all around us,

Dinoflagellates are tiny one-celled creatures that make
a spark of light when disturbed. On some nights, billions of
dinoflagellates can cause the ocean to sparkle with each wave.
Scientists do not fully understand all the ways
that these creatures use their light.

many we haven't even discovered yet,

Over three-quarters of all the animals in the open ocean
make their own light. Scientists are still discovering
more bioluminescent creatures every year. They already know
about thousands of different bioluminescent *species*
(kinds of living things), from tiny bacteria to beetles, worms,
snails, sea stars, and even sharks!

each a part of our extraordinary world.

*Biodiversity* is a word for all the different
types of species that you would find in one place.
Every unique creature helps to keep our world healthy.

So always look,

The common piddock is a type of clam that makes its
home by drilling into rocks. Through bioluminescence,
it glows blue-green around the edges. Although they are
rarely eaten today, these clams would light up the hands
and mouths of those who once ate them.

really look,

If we used less light, what could we see?

Some places have too much human-made
light at night. Creatures living in or passing through
these places can be disrupted by this *light pollution*.
In places with less light, bioluminescence
can sometimes be seen by astronauts in space.

when it's dark out.

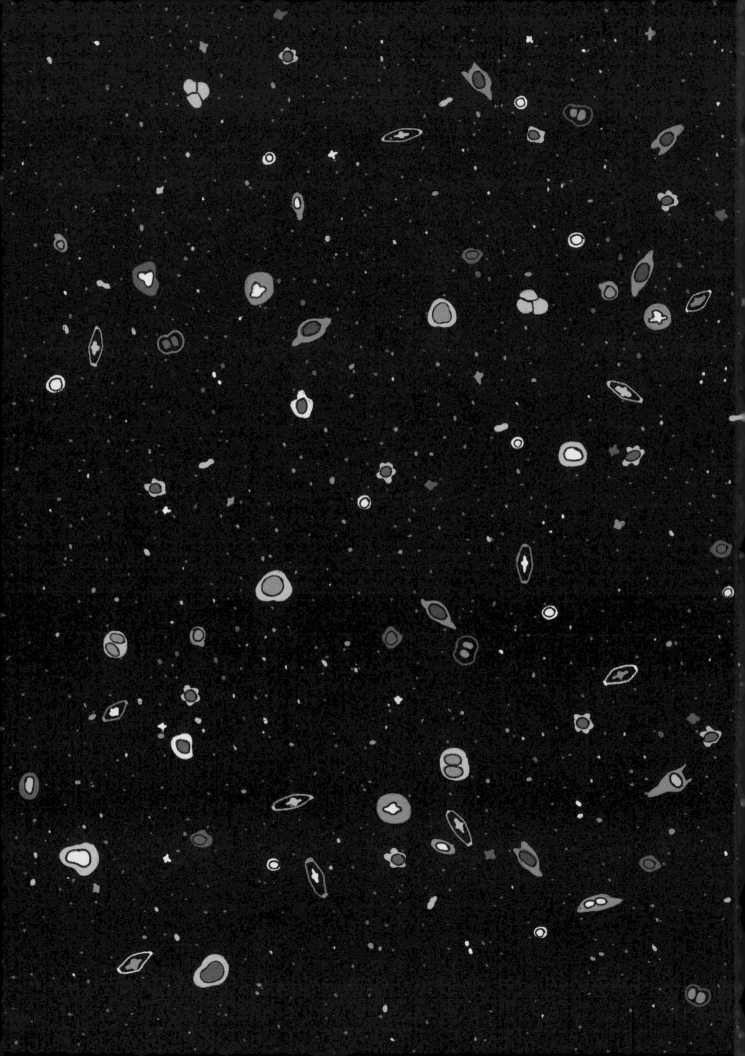